First World War
and Army of Occupation
War Diary
France, Belgium and Germany

52 DIVISION
157 Infantry Brigade,
Brigade Trench Mortar Battery
1 May 1918 - 31 December 1918

WO95/2898/5

The Naval & Military Press Ltd
www.nmarchive.com
Published in association with The National Archives

Published by

The Naval & Military Press Ltd

Unit 10 Ridgewood Industrial Park,

Uckfield, East Sussex,

TN22 5QE England

Tel: +44 (0) 1825 749494

www.naval-military-press.com

www.nmarchive.com

This diary has been reprinted in facsimile from the original. Any imperfections are inevitably reproduced and the quality may fall short of modern type and cartographic standards.

© Crown Copyright
Images reproduced by permission of The National Archives, London, England, 2015.

Contents

Document type	Place/Title	Date From	Date To
Heading	WO95/2898-5		
Heading	52nd Division 157th Infy Bde 157th Lt. Trench Mortar Bty Jan 1919		
War Diary	Field	01/01/1919	31/01/1919
War Diary	War Diary May 1918 No. 10 Vol I		
War Diary	Buigny St. Maclou (Ref Abbeville 1/20000)	01/05/1918	03/05/1918
War Diary	Etaples	04/05/1918	04/05/1918
War Diary	Aire	05/05/1918	07/05/1918
War Diary	Ref Map Maroeuil 1/20000	08/05/1918	31/05/1918
Heading	War Diary No 11 Vol. 1 June 1918		
War Diary	Ref Map Maroeuil 1.20000	01/06/1918	21/06/1918
War Diary	Cubitt Camp Neuville St Vaast	22/06/1918	29/06/1918
War Diary	Ref Map Maroeuil 1.20000	30/06/1918	30/06/1918
Heading	War Diary July 1918 No 12 Vol 1		
War Diary	Ref Map Maroeuil 1/20000 and La Targette 1/20000	01/07/1918	19/07/1918
War Diary	Ref Map France 36b 1/40000 Raimbert	20/07/1918	30/07/1918
War Diary	Ref Map Lens 1/100000	31/07/1918	31/07/1918
Heading	157th T.M.B War Diary For August 1918 No-1 Vol-2		
War Diary	Ref Map Maroeuil 1/20000	01/08/1918	22/08/1918
War Diary	Ref Map France 51 B.SE	23/08/1918	31/08/1918
Heading	157th T.M. Bty War-Diary For Month Of September 1918 No 2 Vol 2		
War Diary	Ref Map France 51b & 57c	01/09/1918	16/09/1918
War Diary	57c NE	16/09/1918	30/09/1918
Heading	War Diary 157 TMB Vol II No for October 1918		
War Diary	Cambrai	01/10/1918	06/10/1918
War Diary	Nr Moeuvres	06/10/1918	07/10/1918
War Diary	Liencourt	08/10/1918	18/10/1918
War Diary	Mont.St Eloi	19/10/1918	19/10/1918
War Diary	Henin Lietard	20/10/1918	20/10/1918
War Diary	Wagnonville	21/10/1918	23/10/1918
War Diary	Flines-Lez-Raches	24/10/1918	26/10/1918
War Diary	Landas	27/10/1918	27/10/1918
War Diary	Lecelles	28/10/1918	31/10/1918
Miscellaneous	Army Form W, 3759		
War Diary		01/11/1918	30/11/1918
War Diary	Field	01/12/1918	31/12/1918

W095/28985
W095/28985

52ND DIVISION
157TH INFY BDE

157TH LT. TRENCH MORTAR BTY

JAN 1919

Army Form C. 2118.

157 T. M. Battery WAR DIARY for January 1919.
or
INTELLIGENCE SUMMARY.
(Erase heading not required.)

Instructions regarding War Diaries and Intelligence Summaries are contained in F. S. Regs., Part II. and the Staff Manual respectively. Title pages will be prepared in manuscript.

Place	Date	Hour	Summary of Events and Information	Remarks and references to Appendices
Field	1/1/19		Billeted at Tibiaux about 15 Belgium and France.	
	1st to 4th		Usual Training Parades.	
	5th		Church Parade.	
	6th to 11th		Usual Training Parades.	
	12th		Cleaning up equipment and preparing for Brig. Ceremonial Parade.	
	13th		Battery attended Brig. Ceremonial Parade and took part in practise for Corps Commander's Parade on 16th inst.	
	14th		Usual Training Parades.	
	15th		Proceeded to and made use of Rifle Range.	
	16th to 18th		Usual Training Parades.	
	19th		Church Parade.	
	20th to 21st		Usual Parades.	
	22nd		Proceeded to and made use of Rifle Range.	
	23rd to 30th			
	31st		Usual Training Parades.	

J. C. Adams
Capt.
O.C. 157 T. M. Battery.

157th L.T.M. Bty

WAR DIARY - MAY 1918.

No 18 - VOL. I

Army Form C. 2118.

WAR DIARY
or
INTELLIGENCE SUMMARY.
(Erase heading not required.)

Instructions regarding War Diaries and Intelligence Summaries are contained in F.S. Regs., Part II. and the Staff Manual respectively. Title pages will be prepared in manuscript.

Place	Date	Hour	Summary of Events and Information	Remarks and references to Appendices
BURGHT ST MARLOU (HARDEVILLE YEANE)	1/3/18 5/3/18 3/18		Battery in billets. Gun Training. Battery Parade. Gas Chamber. Gun Training	
ETAPLES	4/5/18		Battery marched from BURGHT at 0830 to TROYELLES. Entrained at NOYELLES at 1230. Arrived at ETAPLES at 1430. Detrained at ETAPLES & proceeded to No. 9 Rest Camp.	
AIRE	5/5/18 6/5/18 7/5/18		Battery entrained at ETAPLES at 0600 and proceeded to AIRE. Arrived AIRE 1730 & proceeded to FRENCH BARRACKS. Battery Parade - 4 hours Gun Training. Entrained at AIRE at 1800 with 155th Inf. Bde. & proceeded to MARCHE VIC.	
REF. MAP. MARCHE VIC. 1/10,000.	8/5/18 9/5/18 10/5/18 15/5/18 16/5/18		Arrived MAMETZ 0700 and proceeded to FORT VENUS. Relieved 163 L.T.M.B. at 2300 on WITHERNAL sector by No line. 3 guns attached to Right Battalion. 2 guns attached Left Battalion. 2 guns in reserve at Battery H.Q. Battery in line. All ammunition examined & cleaned. Defence Scheme approved by Battalion Commander. Registration on S.O.S. lines carried out. Relieved by 156 L.T.M.B. at 2000 & proceeded to CUSSETT CAMP - MEUVILLE ST VAAST.	

WAR DIARY
or
INTELLIGENCE SUMMARY.

Army Form C. 2118.

(Erase heading not required.)

Place	Date	Hour	Summary of Events and Information	Remarks and references to Appendices
REF WAR	17/10		Relieved 155 L.T.M.B. on left sector 32nd Div. sector. 51 regiment 157 Inf. Brigade 3 guns attached to Right Battalion, 3 guns attached to Left Battalion & 2 guns in reserve at Battery H.Q. at T.13 b.55.	
MARCEUIL	18/10 to		Battery in the line. All ammunition examined & cleaned. S.O.S. line checked. Gun in TOAST TRENCH removed to new emplacement.	
	19/10			
	20/10		Work carried on Ammunition Dumps. Visit of Corps. Commander.	
1/10000.	21/10		Work continued in ammunition Dumps. No 1 Gun removed from Right Batt sector	
	22/10		to T.16.a.2.6	
	23/10		Work continued in ammunition Dumps.	
	24/10			
	25/10		Relieved by 163 R.T.M.B. at 20.00 & proceeded to CUBITT CAMP - NEUVILLE ST. VAAST.	
	26/10		10.00 Battery proceeded to Divisional Baths & men issued with clean clothing.	
	27/10		Reveille 06.30 Battery Parade 06.30-07.00 Physical Training 09.00-12.00 Musketry (range/grenades) Gun drill drill. Trench mortar drill 14.00-15.30 Sig. Training. Trench mortar drill	
			Reveille 06.30 Battery Parade 06.30-07.00 Physical Training 09.00-12.00	
	28/10		Musketry (range of fire) Trench mortar drill 14.00-15.30 Gas Training	
			& close order drill	

Army Form C. 2118.

WAR DIARY
or
INTELLIGENCE SUMMARY
(Erase heading not required.)

Place	Date	Hour	Summary of Events and Information	Remarks and references to Appendices
Ref. Map. MARSEILLE 14,000/1	29/3		Reveille 0530.Ватон Parade 0630-0730 Physical Training 0800-1200 Musketry (Range Practice) Local Musketry Instructors Tactical Exercise 1400-1530 Close Order Drill Travel Tactical Drill	
	30/3		Reveille 0530. Battery Parade 0630-0700 Physical Training 0800-1200 Musketry (Range Practice) Local Musketry Tactical Exercise	
	31/3		Reveille 0530. Battery Parade 0630-0700 Physical and Training 0800-1200 Travel Mortar, Dummy Loading 1430-1600 Lecture Training under Bn. Res. Officers	

A M Bowman
Capt
OC 151 LTMB

WAR-DIARY JUNE-1918

No.11 VOL.1.

William
Capt
a/O.C. 157th L.T.M.B.

Army Form C. 2118.

WAR DIARY
or
INTELLIGENCE SUMMARY.
(Erase heading not required.)

Instructions regarding War Diaries and Intelligence Summaries are contained in F. S. Regs., Part II. and the Staff Manual respectively. Title pages will be prepared in manuscript.

Place	Date	Hour	Summary of Events and Information	Remarks and references to Appendices
Ref Map MARŒUIL 1:20,000	1/5	Saturday	CUBITT CAMP. Battery Paraded 0630-0700 Physical training. 0700-1200 Musketry Practice & Gunnery Firing from Trench Mortars. 1400-1500 Gas training	
	2/5	Sunday	CUBITT CAMP	
	3/5	Monday	Relieved 156 T.M.B. 8 guns in the line. 3 guns with Right Battalion. 3 with Left Bn.	
	4/5	Tuesday	Ammunition required + C.O.S. lines checked.	
	5/5	Wednesday	Usual Routine.	
	6/5	Thursday	Usual Routine.	
	7/5	Friday	10 Rounds fired on Enemy T.M. emplacement at B5 central. Effect good.	
	8/5	Saturday	Usual Routine	
	9/5	Sunday	Withdrawn from front line. Right Section 4 guns to [illegible]. Left Section 3 guns to [illegible]	

Army Form C. 2118.

WAR DIARY
or
INTELLIGENCE SUMMARY.
(Erase heading not required.)

Instructions regarding War Diaries and Intelligence Summaries are contained in F. S. Regs., Part II. and the Staff Manual respectively. Title pages will be prepared in manuscript.

Place	Date	Hour	Summary of Events and Information	Remarks and references to Appendices
Bt Map MARŒUIL 1.29000	10/5	Monday	Work on new gun Pits. Right sector registered	
	11/5	Tuesday	Work on new gun Pits.	
	12/5	Wednesday	Usual gun Pit routine. Work continued on new gun Pits. 110 Rounds Ammunition added to Right Section	
	13/5	Thursday	Usual gun Pit routine. Work continued on new gun positions. Junin VANCOUVER ROAD registered.	
	14/5	Friday	Usual gun Pit routine.	
	15/5	Saturday	Usual gun Pit routine.	
	16/5	Sunday	" " " "	
	17/5	Monday	" " " "	
	18/5	Tuesday	" " " " Pte Laing wounded by shrapnel.	
	19/5	Wednesday	Work done to new forward positions to be used in event of a raid by our troops on enemy.	
	20/5	Thursday	Usual Routine.	
	21/5	Friday	Relieved by 155 L.T.M.B. in right sector of line & proceeded to CORPS CAMP	
COBITT CAMP NEUVILLE ST VAAST	22/5	Saturday	Battery at Baths. Bath issued with clean underclothing.	

Army Form C. 2118.

WAR DIARY
or
INTELLIGENCE SUMMARY.
(Erase heading not required.)

Instructions regarding War Diaries and Intelligence Summaries are contained in F. S. Regs., Part II. and the Staff Manual respectively. Title pages will be prepared in manuscript.

Place	Date	Hour	Summary of Events and Information	Remarks and references to Appendices
CURITT CAMP NEUVILLE ST VAAST	23/6/18	Sunday	Reveille 0700. All equipment scrubbed & brass parts polished.	
"	24/6/18	Monday	0815 fight parade. 0800-0900 Physical training. 1000-1230 Training in use of equipment. 1400 Photo & parade for whole Bty. 2045 fight Parade.	
"	25/6/18	Tuesday	0815 fight Parade. 0830-0900 Physical Training. 1600-1230 Training. 2045 fight Parade.	
"	26/6/18	Wednesday	" " "	
"	27/6/18	Thursday	" 10.00-12.00 Training in &c (Coy or gun Drills) "	
"	28/6/18	Friday	" 1030-1030 Lectures. 1030-1230 Gun order Drill. 2045 fight Parade.	
"	29/6/18	Saturday	1400 Parade for Inspection of C.B.R. at Ross Camp. 2045 fight Parade.	
"	29/6/18	Sunday	0815 fight parade. 0830-0900 Physical Drill. 1000-1230 Training of gun drill and bill. 2045 fight Parade.	
Ref Map MAROEUIL 1/20,000	30/6/18	Sunday	157 M.M. B. Return 1567-1743. 1 Divisional left lentre. 6 guns in line. Two new pits under construction for two guns not present in Divisional Area. Battery H.Qs.	

J. K. Wilson, Capt.
O.C. B. 157 L.F.M. Battery

WAR·DIARY
JULY·1918
N°12·VOL1

WAR DIARY
or
INTELLIGENCE SUMMARY.

Army Form C. 2118.

Place	Date	Hour	Summary of Events and Information	Remarks and references to Appendices
Ref Maps Maroeuil 1/20,000 and LA TARGETTE A/4 1/10,000	1/8		Battery in MERICOURT position. Usual Trench Routine	
	2/7/18		6 guns in line. Bty H.Q. at T.13.d.4.3.	
	3/7/18		2 guns in right Battalion subsector withdrawn from BLUE LINE to BLACK LINE. Usual trench routine.	
			All gun reported in S.O.S. lines. Salvage of ammunition in clumps in BLUE LINE area continued. Usual Trench Routine.	
	5/7/18 6/7/18		Salvage of ammunition in BLUE LINE dumps continued. Improvements on gun pits carried out. Usual trench routine.	
	7/7/18		2 positions for reserve guns pits in BROWN LINE. Salvage of ammunition and improvement of pits continued. Usual Trench routine.	
	8/7/18		Salvage of ammunition from BLUE LINE and improvement of pits continued. Construction of pits in BROWN LINE forwarded on. Usual trench routine.	
	9/7/18 14/7/18 15/7/18		3 guns in right sub-sector relieved by 156"T.M.B and withdrawn to BROWN LINE & reserve position in BROWN LINE then taken over by 156"T.M.B.	
	16/7/18 to 17/7/18		Position of 5 guns held in BROWN LINE. Work connected in their positions. Salvage of ammunition continued. Usual Trench routine.	
	18/7/18		Relieved by 155"T.M.B. & proceeded to CUBBITT CAMP — MENVILLE ST. VAAST.	
	19/7/18		Battery moved to Billets at MONT ST. ELOI	

WAR DIARY
or
INTELLIGENCE SUMMARY

Army Form C. 2118.

(Erase heading not required.)

Instructions regarding War Diaries and Intelligence Summaries are contained in F. S. Regs., Part II. and the Staff Manual respectively. Title pages will be prepared in manuscript.

Place	Date	Hour	Summary of Events and Information	Remarks and references to Appendices
Ref. MAP 40/B			Battery arrived at ST. ELOI station at 0200. Battery entrained at 1000 & detrained at 1530 at CAROINE RICOUART. Battery marched to billets at RAIMBERT.	
FRANCE 36R 1/40,000 RAIMBERT	21/8		Cleaning of Gun Equipment etc. Church Parade 1500.	
	22/8		Battery Parade 0830–1100 Physical Training, Gun Drill, Gas Training, Stokes Mortar Drill.	
	23/8		Battery Parade 0830–1200 Physical Training. Close Order Drill. Musketry, Stokes Mortar Drill.	
	24/8		Battery Parade 0830–1200 Physical Training. Close Order Drill. Stokes Mortar Drill.	
	25/8		Battery Parade 0830–1200 Physical Training. T.M. tactical exercise. Track made up to FrtRd. Annual training inspected by Bde. T.O.	
	26/8		Battery Parade 0830–1200 Physical Training. Gun drill. Musketry Drill. Route march.	
	27/8		Battery Parade 0830–1200 Physical Training. Close Order Drill. Gun training. Stokes mortar Drill.	
	28/8		Cleaning of Gun material. Church Parade 1100.	
	29/8		Battery Parade 0830–1200 Physical Training. Y.M. Lecture. Licence wing Dummy Ammunition	
	30/8		0800 Battery moved with Bde. to BOIS d'HOUDAIN arriving 1530 at Bivouacary for the night.	
Ref. MAP LENS 1/100,000	31/8		1930 Battery moved with BDE to MADAGASCAR CAMP – ECURIE arriving 1930.	

AhBowman
Capt
OC 1577 hB

A9092. Wt. W12639/M1193F 750,000. 1/17. D.D & L., Ltd. Forms/C2118/14.

157th = T.M.B
=251

WAR-DIARY for AUGUST-1918.

No. = 1
VOL = 2

John Miller Lt.
for O.C. 157 T.M.B

Army Form C. 2118.

WAR DIARY
or
INTELLIGENCE SUMMARY.
(Erase heading not required.)

Instructions regarding War Diaries and Intelligence Summaries are contained in F. S. Regs., Part II. and the Staff Manual respectively. Title pages will be prepared in manuscript.

Place	Date	Hour	Summary of Events and Information	Remarks and references to Appendices
1/1 HQrs Margueil Farm	1/8/18		Relieved 3rd Ammn 10th Canadian T.M.B. and 1 Sunn 15b.T.M.B. in line Offoy Sector	
	2/8/18		Informed him employments. Accident to man in T's him pit	
	3/8/18		Ammunition checks and cleaned. Routine as usual.	
	4/8/18		Ranges firing: routine as usual	
	5/8/18		Routine as usual	
	16/8/18		Relieved in line by 2nd & 1 T.M.B. Spent night in Ecourdes	
	17/8/18		Moved to Chateau de la Ture	
	18/8/18		Cleaned equipment	
	19/8/18		Training commenced	
	20/8/18		Training in Livesops	
	21/8/18		Left Chateau de la Ture for "Y. Huts" opp. 4th Division	
	22/8/18		Apres les Divisions resting.	
	23/8/18		Moved from Apres les Divisions to Bella court	
1/1 HQrs Front line 8/12- 24/8/18	23/8/18		Moved from Bella court to Venen for operations	
	25/8/18		Operations attack on Venen	
			Consolidation	

Army Form C. 2118.

WAR DIARY
or
INTELLIGENCE SUMMARY.
(Erase heading not required.)

Instructions regarding War Diaries and Intelligence Summaries are contained in F. S. Regs., Part II. and the Staff Manual respectively. Title pages will be prepared in manuscript.

Place	Date	Hour	Summary of Events and Information	Remarks and references to Appendices
Wytsch.	26/10		Operations: Cruxstradlin	
France 5¹ B.I.E	27/10		attack on Frontani Grivelles	
	1st & 2nd/10		Relieved by 57th Division and left for Herental	
	28/10		Herental: resting	
	29/10		Herental: reorganising	
	30 & 31/10		" "	

John Stiller ?/??
for O.C. 157 T.M.B

157th T.M. Bty.

War-Diary for Month of September 1916

No 2
Vol: 2

[signature]
for O.C. 157th T.M. Bty

WAR DIARY
or
INTELLIGENCE SUMMARY.
(Erase heading not required.)

Army Form C. 2118.

Instructions regarding War Diaries and Intelligence Summaries are contained in F. S. Regs., Part II. and the Staff Manual respectively. Title pages will be prepared in manuscript.

Place	Date	Hour	Summary of Events and Information	Remarks and references to Appendices
Ref Map	1.9.18		Battery moved & Bivouac'd near Percotes & Heilly Hill.	
FRANCE	2.9.18		Battery moved into Bivouac in neighbourhood of Buire Court	
57C	3.9.18		Battery advanced with 6th A.I. Bde to attack QUEANT & PRONVILLE and part of HINDENBURG Line in - Shelton attached 5th A.L.I. 2 batteries attached 7th A.I. Remainder of Battery in Bde reserve. All objectives were taken without opposition. Battery then proceeded to occupy MELBOURNE STREET	
57C	4.9.18 & 7.9.18		Brigade in Corps Support. Battery occupied MELBOURNE STREET	
	7.9.18 & 14.9.18		Battery Bivouac'd with Brigade & Horses in neighbourhood of CROIXELLES. Battery re-organised & receives reinforcements. 2 hour training per day. Special Training or reinforcements. Four Salvage work per day.	
57 M15	16.9.18		Battery relieved 173rd T.M.B. in INCHY SECTOR. Shelton attached right Battalion (57 A.L.I.) 3 Mortars & Flashed left Battalion (6 A.L.I.)	
	16.9.18 & 19.9.18		Battery fired nightly on enemy M.G. - got results. Stand to & S.O.S. on 17/9/18 with good results. Relieved by 5th Mortars T.M. B. 19/8/18 & proceeded to Bivouac in neighbourhood of MOREUIL.	
	20.9.18 & 25.9.18		Resting & re-organising. 2 Mortars provided with 6 A.L.I. on 22/9/18 to be attached to 150th Regt. Amn. in the line in MC.INNES sector.	
	26.9.18		Battery warned to line to register for barrage in attack by 157th Bde on CANAL du NORD.	
57C.& B	27.9.18		157th Bde the attacked CANAL DU NORD and further objectives. All Mortars conformed to Battery barrage & further bombarded individually. Battery Canal de Nord - 2 Mortars provided with 6 A.L.I. after crossing the Canal.	
			1st Setting up position for the Bde attack. 2 Mortars attacked each battalion holding line of CANAL du NORD - Salvage work daily.	
	23.9.18 & 30.9.18		Battery assisted in some role. 2 Mortars	

157. T M B

WAR DIARY. 1st October 1918.

157TH LIGHT TRENCH MORTAR BATTERY

Vol II
No 3

Army Form C. 2118.

WAR DIARY
or
INTELLIGENCE SUMMARY.
(Erase heading not required.)

Instructions regarding War Diaries and Intelligence Summaries are contained in F.S. Regs., Part II. and the Staff Manual respectively. Title pages will be prepared in manuscript.

Place	Date	Hour	Summary of Events and Information	Remarks and references to Appendices
CAMBRAI	1/10/18 to 4/10/18		Battery with 157 Bde in support of 155 Bde in neighbourhood of CANTIGNEUR MILL	
	4/10/18		157 Bde relieved 155 Bde in line south of PROVILLE 157 J.h.B. relieved 155 J.h.B – 3 batteries attd left batt. (S.H.U.) 2 batteries attd right batt. (6 H.U.)	
	6/10/18		– Enemy in lt's were "stonked" at intervals during the night. 157 J.h.B relieved by 172 J.h.B on night 5/6 October.	
Mn MOEUVRES	10/10/18		Battery marched to known area in HINDENBURG LINE near MOEUVRES	
	7/10/18		Battery marched to VAUX - VRAUCOURT and entrained for LIENCOURT	
LIENCOURT	8/10/18 to 18/10/18		Battery in billets at LIENCOURT. Four crews trained carried out daily. Special attention paid during training to methods of firing mortar without mounting. Four tactical schemes carried out in co-operation with infantry.	
MONT ST ELOI	19/10/18		Battery moved with 157 Bde from LIENCOURT to billets at MONT ST ELOI	
HENIN LIETARD	20/10/18		Battery moved with 157 Bde from MONT ST ELOI to billets at HENIN LIETARD	
WAGNONVILLE	21/10/18		Battery moved with 157 Bde from HENIN LIETARD to WAGNONVILLE	
	22/10/18		Battery cleaned up kit and equipment	

Army Form C. 2118.

WAR DIARY
or
INTELLIGENCE SUMMARY.

(Erase heading not required.)

Instructions regarding War Diaries and Intelligence Summaries are contained in F.S. Regs., Part II. and the Staff Manual respectively. Title pages will be prepared in manuscript.

Place	Date	Hour	Summary of Events and Information	Remarks and references to Appendices
WAGNONVILLE	23/10		Training - 2 hours attached to each Battn of 157 Bde to co-operate in tactical schemes	
FLINES -	24/10		Battery moved with 157 Bde to billets in FLINES-LEZ- RACHES	
LEZ-RACHES	25/10		Battery on working party, repairing roads in FLINES	
	26/10		Training carried out for four hours	
LANDAS	27/10		Battery moved with 157 Bde to billets at LANDAS	
LEEELLES	28/10		Battery moved with 157 Bde to billets at LEEELLES	
	29/10		Battery cleaning kit and equipment	
	30/10		Battery training for four hours	
	31/10		Battery training. 2 howitzers attached to 1/6 HLI for tactical schemes	

A.W. Bowman
Capt
O.C. 157 V.L.B.

(7 27 29) W90—P51527 200,000 4/18 HWV(P94)   Army Form W. 3759.

FORMATION _____   191 __ .

Leave Return for month ending 28th _____

(To be rendered to A.G., G.H.Q., by 3rd of every month by Corps and by Formations to whom leave allotment is made by G.H.Q.)

FORMATION	"X" No. of other ranks without leave				"Y" No. of other ranks without leave for over 15 months, who are debarred				"Z" No. of other ranks awarded but not yet presented with medals who have not had leave for over 10 months, and are not debarred under column "Y"	NOTES
	"A" Over 18 months	"B" Over 15 months	"C" Over 12 months	"D" Over 10 months	"V"	"P"	"O"	Total debarred		
(1)	(2)	(3)	(4)	(5)	(6)	(7)	(8)	(9)	(10)	

Notes:
(1) Corps returns will show figures for Divisions and Corps Troops separately.
(2) Numbers to be included in "B," "C" and "D."
(3) Numbers to be included in "C" and "D."
(4) Numbers to be included in "D."
(6) "V" = Venereal disease.
(7) "P" = Punishment.
(8) "O" = Not eligible for other causes.
(9) **Numbers under "Y" will not be included in numbers under "X."**
(10) Includes the following medals:—V.C., M.C., D.C.M., M.M., M.S.M., Albert Medal and Edward Medal. Numbers under "Z" will be included in numbers under "X."

To

Signed,

WAR DIARY
or
INTELLIGENCE SUMMARY.
(Erase heading not required.)

Army Form C. 2118.

FOR NOVEMBER.

Place	Date	Hour	Summary of Events and Information	Remarks and references to Appendices
NOVEMBER 1 to 3			Billeted at LESCELLES	
	4th		Battery moved to LA CROISETTE and relieved 23 Bde L.T.M.B. and four guns moved into the line with L.H.L.S	
	9th		Battery moved to ODOMEZ	
	10	" " " HARCHIES		
	11	" " " VACRESSE. Armistice signed - Two guns with 5th H.L.S returned to Vesgo Battery. - Two guns attached to 5th N.Z.B. at ERBISOETH.		
	11 to 14?		Overhauling & cleaning material and General Training Parade. 5th N.Z.L.I relieved by 6th N.Z.B - Two guns went to relieve those who were out with 5th N.Z.B.	
	14-20		General Training Parade.	
	21st		Inspection of Material & Transport by B.G.C.	
	21-24		General Training Parade.	
	25		Moved from VACRESSE to TILLES at K.I.D.7.10 sheet 45 France & Belgium	
	29		Inspection by B.G.C. of Material & Unit Transport	
	30			

J.S. Allen Capt RFA
157 L.T.M.B.

Army Form C. 2118.

WAR DIARY
or
INTELLIGENCE SUMMARY.

Mr 157 L.T.M.B. 52 Division

(Erase heading not required.)

Instructions regarding War Diaries and Intelligence Summaries are contained in F. S. Regs., Part II. and the Staff Manual respectively. Title pages will be prepared in manuscript.

December 1918.

Place	Date	Hour	Summary of Events and Information	Remarks and references to Appendices
Field	1st-		Billeted in school BRUYERE Sheet 45 BELGIUM & FRANCE. K.I.d.7.10	
	10		Usual training parades, scrubbing and cleaning up equipment and practising for Infantry Brigade Demonstration	
	11		Right Section of Battery took part in 157 Inf. Brig. Demonstration. Battery moved to new billets at T.16.d.2.4. Sheet 45 (BELGIUM and FRANCE)	
	12-		Usual training parades, two hours daily and class taken in French one hour daily	
	14			
	15		Cleaning and polishing equipment for inspection by Divisional Commander.	
	16		Inspection by Divisional Commander.	
	17-24		Usual training parades.	
	25		Christmas Day.	
	29		Billets inspected by B.G.C.	
	26-31		Usual training parades.	

2-1-1919.

A.W. Brown Capt.
Commdg 157 L.T.M.B.

www.ingramcontent.com/pod-product-compliance
Lightning Source LLC
Chambersburg PA
CBHW081505160426
43193CB00014B/2598